THOUGHTS CONCERNING THE KING

"Thoughts"

Thoughts Concerning the King

ELIZABETH PRENTISS

CURIOSMITH
MINNEAPOLIS

Published by Curiosmith.
Minneapolis, Minnesota.
Internet: curiosmith.com.

Previously published by H. M. CALDWELL Co. in 1890.

Supplementary content, layout and cover design:
Copyright © 2015 Charles J. Doe.

ISBN 9781941281550

CONTENTS

CONTENTS *(Continued)*

These selections were originally made for private use. By permission of Dr. Prentiss they are now published in their present form, and with the hope that they may prove as helpful to others as they have already been to the compiler.

M. B. L.

Jesus a Saviour

ONE hour with Jesus; how its peace outweighs
The banishment of earthly love and praise;
How dearer far, emptied of self, to lie
Low at His feet, and catch, perchance His eye,
Alike content when He may give or take,
The sweet, the bitter, welcome for His sake.

THERE is certainly enough in our Saviour, if we
only open our eyes that we may see it, to solve every
doubt and satisfy every longing of the heart; and He
is willing to give it in full measure.

IF a glimpse of our Saviour here on earth can be so
refreshing, so delightful, what will it be in Heaven?

SOMETIMES when I feel almost sure that the Saviour
has accepted and forgiven me, and that I belong

to Him, I can only walk my room repeating over and over again, how wonderful! And then when my mind strives to take in this love of Christ, it seems to struggle in vain with its own littleness, and falls back weary and exhausted, to wonder again at the heights and depths which surpass its comprehension.

ALONE WITH GOD

Into my closet fleeing, as the dove
    Doth homeward flee,
I haste away to ponder o'er Thy love,
    Alone with Thee!

In the dim wood, by human ear unheard,
    Joyous and free,
Lord! I adore Thee, feasting on Thy Word,
    Alone with Thee!

Amid the busy city, thronged and gay,
    But One I see,
Tasting sweet peace, as unobserved I pray
    Alone with Thee!

Oh, happy life! Life hid with Christ in God!
    So making me
At home, and by the wayside, and abroad,
    Alone with Thee.

I HAVE felt that if, in the course of my life, I should be the means of leading one soul to the Saviour, it would be worth staying in this world for no matter how many years.

WHAT a Friend and Saviour we have, and how He comes to meet us on the sea, if we attempt to walk there in faith.

A SOUL that has known what it is to live to Christ can be happy only in Him.

I HAVE always felt a peculiar love for the passage that describes the walk to Emmaus. I have tried to analyze the feeling of pleasure which it invariably sheds over my heart when dwelling upon it, especially the words, "Jesus Himself drew near and went with them." And then, "He made as though He would go farther," but yielded to their urgent "Abide with us."

AT JESUS' FEET

There is a spot where templed souls
  May find a dear retreat;
They fly from sin and self, and lie
  At Jesus' feet.

In vain upon their heads the storms
  Of life may rudely beat,
Grief cannot harm the soul that lies
  At Jesus' feet.

My soul, upon life's dizzy heights
  Beware to take thy seat,
Leave not the valley, but abide
  At Jesus' feet.

Wouldst thou in peace, and joy, and love,
  And gladness, stand complete?
Seek it in penitence and faith,
  At Jesus' feet.

Yes, I love everybody; that crowning joy has come to me at last. Christ in my soul; He is mine; I am as conscious of it as that my husband and children are mine; and His spirit flows forth from mine in the calm peace of a river, whose banks are green with grass, and glad with flowers.

I BELIEVE God does reveal Himself and His truth to those who are willing to know it.

WHAT CHRIST CAN BE

OH that some faithful soul could tell
　　What Jesus Christ can be,
To the distracted soul that sinks
　　In sorrow's briny sea,
And casts a last despairing look
　　To His wide sympathy.

No mother's hand with clasp so soft,
　　So true, so kind can press,
And of the gentle, loving tone
　　A mother's voice has less;
Yea, she that bare thee is but rough
　　To Jesus' tenderness.

Come and behold what Jesus is;
　　Into His gracious ear
Pour all the story of thy grief,
　　Whisper thine every fear,
And on His sympathizing breast
　　Weep out thine every tear.

Then first the risen Son of God
　　Shall unto thee be known,
Then only canst thou feel His heart

    Respond to every groan,
And echo to the bursting sigh,
    The plaintive, helpless moan.

Ah, joyful hearts that know not grief,
    Can never Jesus know;
He must be learned in darksome nights,
    Where bitter fountains flow,
Where souls are floated off to sea
    By tides of earthly woe.

There have I met Thee, dearest Lord:
    And oh, how passing sweet
Was, to my sinking soul, the sound
    Of Thine approaching feet—
To point Thee out to drowning ones,
    Oh, make me, make me meet!

OH, how true this is; who is so fitted to sing praises to Christ as he who has learned Him in hours of bereavement, disappointment, and despair?

IF we spent more time in thanking God for what He has done for us. He would do more.

THIS is the testimony of all the good books, sermons,

hymns, and memoirs I read—that God's ways are infinitely perfect; that we are to love Him for what He is, and therefore equally as much when He afflicts us as when He prospers us; that there is no real happiness but in doing and suffering His will, and that life is but a scene of probation through which we pass to the real life above.

LET us love Him better and better every day, and count no work for Him too small and unnoticed to be wrought thankfully whenever He gives the opportunity.

HE who has let self go, and lives only for the honor of God, is the free, the happy man. He is no longer a slave, but has the liberty of the sons of God, for "him who honors Me, I will honor."

O CHRIST, I yearn for more of Thee:
Reveal, reveal Thyself to me,
    And satisfy this heart
That would be Thine alone.
    I want Thee wholly, not in part,
    I want to know that mine Thou art,
To know as I am known;

Within this breast Thy love has glowed,
Oh, come and make it Thine abode.

IN proportion to your devotion to the Saviour will be the blessedness of your life.

HOLINESS is not a mere abstraction: it is praying and loving and being consecrate; but it is also the doing kind deeds, speaking friendly words, being in a crowd when we thirst to be alone, and so on, and so on. The study of Christ's life on earth reveals Him to us as incessantly busy, yet taking special seasons for prayer. It seems to me that we should imitate Him in this respect, and when we find ourselves particularly pressed by outward cares and duties, break short off, and withdraw from them till a spiritual tone returns. For we can do nothing well unless we do it consciously for Christ.

I AM persuaded that real meekness dwells deep within the heart, and that it is only to be gained by communion with our blessed Saviour, who, when He was reviled, reviled not again.

THIS is one of the comforts of the Christian: God understands him fully whether he can explain his troubles or not.

THE more I reflect and the more I pray, the more life narrows down to one point—what am I being for Christ, what am I doing for Him? Why do I tell you this? Because the voice of a fellow-traveller always stimulates his brother-pilgrim; what one finds and speaks of and rejoices over, sets the other upon determining to find too. God has been very good to you, as well as to me, but we ought to whisper to each other now and then, "Go on, step faster, step surer, lay hold on the Rock of Ages with both hands."

JESUS BE ALL

O LORD, I know that Thou wilt give to me
   All that I really want;
And yet with heart insatiate and athirst
   For more of Thee I pant.

Bid me long on; help me to strive and pray,
   For I would rather kneel
Rent by conflicting wants, than never thirst
   For Thee, my Lord, to feel.

Give me the prayer of faith, that must prevail;
    Dictate what my poor heart
Shall say to Thee, and how it shall be said,
    Jesus, till mine Thou art.

Come to me with my earliest waking thought,
    Be with me where I go;
Be my last thought at night, and in my dreams
    Thy blessed presence show.

I am so weak, so helpless, Thou so strong;
    Oh, do not let me fall!
My self-despair alone must plead my cause,
    Jesus, be Thou mine all!

THE greatest saint on earth has got to reach Heaven on the same terms as the greatest sinner; unworthy, unfit, good-for-nothing; but saved through grace.

IN proportion to our love to Christ, will be the agony of terror lest we should sin and fall, and so grieve and weary Him.

ONE minute of nearness to the Lord Jesus contains more of delight than years spent in intercourse with any earthly friend.

IF the loss of your fortune gains Christ for you, it will be a beautiful loss.

THE NEW SONG
"And they sang a new song."

THERE is a song I want to sing—
    Or want to learn to sing;
It is a song of praise to Thee,
    Jesus, my Lord and King.

Oh, teach me all its varied notes,
    Its hidden melody,
Till I have learned to sing by heart
    This song of praise to Thee.

I want to sing, while yet on earth,
    The tender, thankful strain
Of saints, who gladly near thy throne,
    Make Thee their song's refrain.

For though I am not yet a saint,
    And though my praises ring
From an encumbered, earthly soul,
    I love the strains they sing.

And well I love, I know I love,

Though truly not as they,
Thee, blessed Jesus, whom I praise
Feebly on earth today.

While there's a song I want to sing—
Or want to learn to sing;
A blessed song of love to Thee,
Jesus, my Lord and King.

IT is not true that as soon as human beings reach a certain point in the divine life, they are snatched out of this; saints move about us and among us every day. They live to be our examples; to be our dearly beloved and cherished ones; to remind us of Heaven, whose spirit they have won; to pray for us, and with us; to inspire and to cheer us. They are saints, but they see not the mark in their foreheads; they wrestle with the powers of the air, and with their own spiritual infirmities; they err sometimes, though sorely against their will, but they are bearing right onward, and are more than conquerors through Him who hath loved them.

COMPLETE IN CHRIST
"Ye are complete in Him."

COMPLETE in Him! oh, Lord, I flee,

Laden with this great thought, to Thee,
With tears and smiles contending, cry,
Are words like these for such as I?

Complete in Him! No word of mine
Is needed, Lord, to perfect Thine;
Wise Master-Builder, let Thy hand
Fashion the fabric Thou hast planned.

Complete in Him! I nothing bring,
Am an imperfect, useless thing;
But human eyes shall joy to see
What God's dear hand shall add to me.

Complete in Him! Oh, longed-for day,
When my poor, sinful heart can say,
Naught in myself, for ruin meet,
In Jesus Christ I stand complete.

I DON'T think the Bible lays down laws about the
order in which God shall grant us His gifts. To one,
He gives repentance first, and faith and love after-
ward; to another, faith and love, and they lead to
repentance. The more we love Him, the more we
see how sinful sin is, and the more sorry we are to
have been guilty of it.

GIVE yourself to Christ. Then ask Him to give you repentance and faith, and everything else you need.

BUT I thought it took a long time, and that people had to read and pray, and get wretched, and then at last they would feel their sins roll off their backs in a great bundle, and go on ever after relieved.

BUT that is not true. The first thing is to believe in Christ, and give yourself to Him, sins and all.

MORE LOVE TO THEE, O CHRIST

1.

MORE love to Thee, O Christ,
    More love to Thee!
Here Thou the prayer I make,
    On bended knee:
This is my earnest plea—
More love, O Christ, to Thee,
    More love to Thee!

2.

Once earthly joy I craved,
    Sought peace and rest;
Now Thee alone I seek,
    Give what is best;

This all my prayer shall be—
More love, O Christ, to Thee,
    More love to Thee!

3.

Let sorrow do its work,
    Send grief and pain,
Sweet are Thy messengers,
    Sweet their refrain,
When they can sing with me—
More love, O Christ, to Thee,
    More love to Thee!

4.

Then shall my latest breath
    Whisper Thy praise,
This be the parting cry
    My heart shall raise;
This still its prayer shall be—
More love, O Christ, to Thee,
    More love to Thee!

I ENTREAT you to turn your eyes away from self, from man, and look to Christ.

LET us never allow aught to come between our hearts and our God.

IT is sweet to be in the sunshine of the Master's smile, but I believe our souls need winter as well as summer, night as well as day.

Jesus a Consoler

THE SAFE PLACE

1.

I WENT to Jesus with a prayer
    Upon a suppliant's knee;
Low at His cross I laid me down,
    Nor asked His face to see,
Yet whispered in His ear the tale
    No mortal ear could bear:
The story of a faithless heart,
    And of its self-despair.

2.

I told Him how my feet had slipped,
    How often gone astray;
How oft my heart refused to love,
    My lips refused to pray.
In stammering words that none but He
    Hearing could understand,
I made complaint of careless work
    Done by a careless hand.

3.

Of wasted hours, of idle words,
    Of love oft waxing dim,
Of silence when a warmer heart
    Had testified of Him.
I owned my weak and selfish ways;
    How often all day long,
Meanings and sighs had filled His ears
    To whom I owed a song.
And what said He? What whispered words
    Responded unto mine.
Did He reproach me? Did His love
    On me refuse to shine?

4.

Nay, thus He spake, and bent Him low
    To reach my anxious ear,
"My child, thou doest well to lie
    As thou art lying here;
I knew thy human weakness, knew
    Each lurking bosom sin,
Knew it, and yet in loving grace
    Thy heart I stooped to win.

5.

"I knew that thou wouldst often fall,
    Poor work for Me wouldst do,
Wouldst give Me only half thy love,
    Give praises faint and few.
And yet I choose thee. Be content;

And since thou canst not fly
To heights by dearer souls attained,
    Let it suffice to lie.

6.

"Here at My feet; it is the place
    To which My loved ones flee;
They find it sweet, and so shalt thou;
    ''Tis a safe place for thee.'"
Yes, it is sweet, and it is safe!
    And here will I abide;
Sinful, and yet forgiven, sad,
    And yet so satisfied.

LET us take our lot in life just as it comes, coura-
geously, patiently, and faithfully, never wondering
at anything the Master does.

WHILE reading tonight that chapter in Mark, where
it speaks of Jesus as walking on the sea, I was inter-
ested in thinking how frequently such scenes occur
in our spiritual passages over the sea which is to
finally land us on the shores of the home for which
we long. "While they were toiling in sowing," Jesus
went to them upon the water and "would have
passed by," till He heard their cries, and then He
manifested Himself unto them, saying, "It is I."

And when He came to them, the wind ceased, and they "wondered." Surely we have often found in our toiling that Jesus was passing by and ready at the first trembling fear to speak the word of love and of consolation, and to give us the needed help, and then to leave us wondering indeed at the infinite tenderness and kindness so unexpectedly vouchsafed for our relief.

I HAVE lived to see that God never was so good to me as when He seemed most severe.

WITH GREAT DELIGHT
"I sat down under His shadow with great delight."
"I will abide under the shadow of the Almighty."

With great delight! Yes, so I sat and rested
   in His shade
When of the burden of the day, and of its
   glare afraid;
I felt myself protected, saved, looked up and
   saw His face,
How beautiful in tenderness, how wonderful
   in grace!

With great delight! Life pressed me sore, I
   knew not where to flee,

In all the world I saw no room, no sphere,
no work for me;
He called me to this sheltered spot, rebuking
my despair,
I went, and oh the joy I found, the peace I
tasted there!

With great delight! A loving friend had
fallen at my side,
My eyes were blinded by my tears, my heart
within me died;
I staggered from the empty world, into this
dear retreat,
And found my bitter grief assuaged, yea,
found my sorrow sweet.

With great delight! My heart is fixed, its
endless wants I know,
Forth from this shelter I henceforth will
never, never go;
Here in the shadow of God's love forever I'll
abide,
So glad, so blest, so sure, so safe; so more
than satisfied!

GOD never places us in any position in which we
cannot grow. We may fancy that He does. We may
fear we are so impeded by fretting petty cares that

we are gaining nothing; but when we are not sending any branches upward, we may be sending roots
downward.

PERHAPS in the time of our humiliation, when
everything seems a failure, we are making the best
kind of progress.

LOOK on and look up; lay hold on Christ with both
your poor, empty hands; let Him do with you what
seemeth Him good; though He slay you, still trust
in Him; and I dare in His name to promise you a
sweeter, better life than you could have known, had
He left you to drink of the full dangerous cups of
unmingled prosperity.

To go back again to the subject of Christ's love for
us, of which I never tire, I want to make you feel
that His sufferers are His happiest, most favored
disciples. What they learn about Him—His piti-
fulness, His unwillingness to hurt us, His haste to
bind up the very wounds He has inflicted—endear
Him so, that at last they burst out into songs of
thanksgiving, that His "donation of bliss" included
in it such donation of pain. Perhaps I have already

said to you, for I am fond of saying it—
The love of Jesus—what it is,
Only His sufferers know.

THEY HAVE BEEN WITH JESUS
"And they took knowledge of them."

HAVE they not been with Jesus? See how their
faces shine
With a radiance unearthly, with a glow
almost divine;
His mark is on their foreheads, His grace is
in their smile,
Every feature is the witness of a spirit without
guile.

They must have been with Jesus, for truly
they alone
Who dwell with Him, can ever catch the
sweetness of His tone,
What tenderness, what earnestness, is
breathed in every note;
What thrills of joy melodious, within its
cadence float.

They have been much with Jesus! no better
proof it needs,
Than the beauty and the kindliness of all
their holy deeds,

Theirs are the hands that minister to want
and to distress,
That into every bitter cup a healing cordial
press.

They have been long with Jesus, within His
blessed school.
They have yielded meek obedience to lesson
and to rule.
The wisdom of their teachings marks the
graces of their speech,
Which guides the meek and ignorant, yet
may the highest reach.

Yes, they have been with Jesus! and counting
all things dross,
Have bent, for His dear sake, beneath the
burden of His cross;
What chastened, humbled souls are theirs,
how unto His akin;
Thrice blessed are ye gracious ones, all
heaven is yours to win.

O IF the unseen presence of Jesus can make the
heart to sing for joy in the midst of its sorrow and
sin here, what will it be to dwell with Him forever.

WE never know, or begin to know, the great Heart that loves us best, till we throw ourselves upon it in the hour of our despair. Friends say and do all they can for us, but they do not know what we suffer or what we need; but Christ who formed, has penetrated the depths of the mother's heart. He pours in the oil that no human hand possesses, and "as one whom his mother comforteth, so will He comfort you."

LAY down this principle as a law—God does nothing arbitrary. If He takes away your health, for instance, it is because He has some reason for doing so; and this is true of everything you value; and if you have real faith in Him, you will not insist on knowing this reason. If you find in the course of daily events, that your self-consecration was not perfect—that is, that your will revolts at His will—do not be discouraged, but fly to your Saviour, and stay in His presence till you obtain the spirit in which He cried in His hour of anguish, "Father, if Thou be willing, remove this cup from me; nevertheless, not my will, but Thine be done."

LOVE is sweet when all goes well, but oh how fearfully exacting it is when separation comes. How many tithes it takes of all we have and are.

WHAT are trials but angels to beckon us nearer to Him.

HOLD ME UP
"Hold Thou me up and I shall be safe."

I CANNOT trust myself, Jesus my Lord,
    Hold Thou me up!
My feet had well-nigh slipped, with Thine own word,
    Hold Thou me up!
Oh, teach me how, and when, and where to go,
The path of safety I entreat to know.

I cannot walk alone; I am a child,
    Hold Thou me up!
And yet to try my strength am oft beguiled;
    Hold Thou me up!
Support me, lead me, keep me in Thy way,
Be Thou my Surety, Thou my Strength and Stay.

Oh, do not let me fall! I cling to Thee;
    Hold Thou me up!
Be merciful in this great strait to me,
    Hold Thou me up!
Let Thy strong hand prevent me; let Thy grace
Carry me safely past this slippery place.

For I have fallen, and I know its pain;
    Hold Thou me up!
Fallen and risen, risen to fall again;
    Hold Thou me up!
My weakness and my helplessness I know;
Hold Thou me up, I will not let Thee go!

MAY our dear Lord bless you abundantly with His sweet presence; I know He will. And yet He has willed it that you should suffer. "Himself hath done it." Oh, how glad He will be when the dispensation of suffering is over, and He can gather His beloved around Him, tearless, free from sorrow and care, and all forever at rest.

WHAT does it matter, after all, from what point of time or space we go home; how we shall smile after we get there, that we ever gave it one moment's thought.

Do not let the thought of what those who love you must suffer in your loss, diminish the peace and joy with which God now calls you to think only of Himself, and the home He has prepared for you. Try to leave them to His kind, tender care. He loves them better than you do; He can be to them more than you have been; He will hear your prayers and all the prayers offered for them, and as one whom his mother comforteth, so will He comfort them. We who shall be left here without you, cannot conceive the joys on which you are to enter, but we know enough to go with you to the very gates of the City, longing to enter in with you to go no more out.

All your tears will soon be wiped away; you will see the King in His beauty; you will see Christ your Redeemer, and realize all He is, and all He has done for you; and how many saints whom you have loved on earth will be standing ready to seize you by the hand and welcome you among them. As I think of these things my soul is in haste to be gone; I long to be set free from sin and self, and to go to the fellowship of those who have done with them forever, and are perfect and entire, wanting nothing.

GO AND TELL JESUS

Oh, aching heart, oh, restless brain,
Go and tell Jesus of thy pain;
He knows thee, loves thee, and His eye
Beams with divinest sympathy.

Go and tell Jesus; human ear
Thy mournful story may not hear;

Keep nothing back, for thee He cares,
His patient heart thy burden bears.

Go and tell Jesus; well He knows
The human heart; its pangs, its throes;
He will not fail thee, He will be
Friend, Comforter, and Peace to thee.

Go and tell Jesus; never yet
Did He a breaking heart forget;
Press closely to His bleeding side,
There, there thou shalt be satisfied.

YOUR little lamb has been spending his first Sunday with the Good Shepherd and other lambs of the flock, and has been as happy as the day is long. Perhaps your two children and mine are claiming kinship together. If they met in a foreign land they would surely claim it for our sakes; why not in the land that is not foreign, and not far off? But still these are not the thoughts to bring you special comfort. "Thy will be done," does the whole.

"IS IT WELL WITH THE CHILD?"

YES, it is well! For he has gone from me,
From my poor care, my human fallacy,

Straight to the Master's school, the Shepherd's love.
Blessed are they whose training is above!
He will grow up in Heaven; will never know
The conflicts that attend our life below.
He from his earliest consciousness shall walk
With Christ Himself in glory; he shall talk
With sinless little children, and his ear
No sound discordant, no harsh word shall hear.
Nay, but I have no words with which to tell
How well it is with him—how well, how well!

I HOPE this golden stair up which your dear boy climbed with "shout and song," is covered with God's angels coming down to bless and comfort you.

DEATH is a blessed thing to the one whom it leads to Christ's kingdom and presence, but oh how terrible for those it leaves panting and weeping behind.

ALL safe at God's right hand! What more can the fondest mother's heart ask than such safety as this?

NEXT to faith in God comes patience; I see that

more and more, and few possess enough of either to enable them to meet the day of bereavement without dismay.

"IS IT WELL WITH THEE?"

Yes, it is well! For while with anguish wild
I gave to God who asked him, my child,
He gave to me strong faith, and peace and joy;
Gave me these blessings when He took my boy.
He gave Himself to me; in boundless grace
Within my deepest depths He took His place;
Made heaven look home-like, made my bleeding heart
In all the grief of other hearts take part;
Brought down my pride, burnt up my hidden dross,
Made me fling down the world and clasp the cross.
Ah, how my inmost soul doth in me swell,
When I declare that all with me is well!

The peaceful fruits of sorrow do not ripen at once; there is a long time of weariness and heaviness while this process is going on; but I do not, will not doubt that you will taste these fruits and find them very sweet. One of the hard things about bereavement is the physical prostration and listlessness, which make it next to impossible to pray and quite impossible to feel the least interest in anything. We must bear this as a part of the pain, believing that it will not last forever, for nothing but God's goodness does.

"GOD's angels coming down on errands sweet,
Our angels going home."

SHE is at home; she is well, she is happy, she will never know a bereavement or a day's illness, or the infirmities and trials of old age; she has got the secret of perpetual youth. The only real comfort is, that God never makes mistakes; that He would not have snatched her from us if He had not had a reason that would satisfy us if we knew it.

WE must not associate anything so unnatural as death with a being so eminently formed for life. We must look beyond, as soon as our tears will let us, to the sphere on which she has been honored to enter in her brilliant youth; to the society of the noblest and the best human beings earth has ever known; to the fullness of life, the perfection of every gift and grace; to congenial employment; to the welcome of Him who has conquered death and brought life and immortality to light.

BUT the shadow of death will not always rest on your home; you will emerge from its obscurity into such a light as they who have never suffered cannot know. We never know, or begin to know, the great Heart that loves us best, till we throw ourselves upon it in the hour of our despair. Friends say and do all they can for us, but they do not know what we suffer or what we need; but Christ, who formed, has penetrated the depths of the mother's heart. He pours in the wine and the oil that no human hand possesses, and "as one whom his mother comforteth, so will He comfort you."

THE SCHOOL

1.

WE are scholars, nothing but scholars,
    Little children at school,
Learning our daily lessons,
    Subject to law and rule.

2.

Life is the School, and the Master
    Is the Man Jesus Christ;
We are His charity scholars,
    His the teaching unpriced.

3.

Slowly we learn, all His patience
    Is hourly put to the test;
But often the slowest and dullest,
    He pities, and loves the best.

4.

Still, we sit at the feet of our Master,
    Very low at His feet,
Study the lessons He sets us,
    Sometimes lessons repeat.

5.

Some of the lessons are pleasant,
    Pleasant and easy to learn;
The page of our task-book simple,
    Simple and easy to turn.

6.

But anon the reading is painful,
    Studied 'mid sighing and tears;
We stammer and falter over it,
    Do not learn it for years.

7.

Yet that is no fault of the Master;
    All His lessons are good;
Only our childish folly
    Leaves them misunderstood.

8.

And still we go on, learning,
    And learning to love our school;
Learning to love our Master,
    Learning to love His rule.

9.

And by and by, we children
    Shall grow into perfect men,
And the loving, patient Master
    From school will dismiss us then.

10.

No more tedious lessons,
    No more sighing and tears,
But a bound into home immortal,
    And blessed, blessed years!

FOR my part I am confounded when I see people hurt and distressed when invited home. How a loving Father must feel when His children shrink back crying, "I have so much to live for," or in other words, so little to die for. It frightens me sometimes to recall such cases.

"AFTER I am dead!" That means, oh ravishing thought! that I shall be in Heaven one day.

NEXT to dying and going home one's self, it must be sweet to accompany a Christian friend down to the very banks of the river. Isn't it strange that after such experiences we can ever again have a worldly thought, or ever lose the sense of the reality of divine things!

GOD delights to try our faith by the conditions in which He places us.

EVERY day I live I see that faith is my only hope as perhaps I never saw it before.

DYING grace is not usually given until it is needed. Death to the disciple of Jesus is only stepping from one room to another and far better room of our Father's house. And how little all the sorrows of the way will seem to us, when we get to our home above.

YOU never will be really happy till Christ becomes your dearest and most intimate friend.

FAITH is His—unbelief ours. No process of reasoning can soothe a mother's empty, aching heart, or bring Christ into it to fill up all that great waste room. But faith can. And faith is His gift; a gift to be won by prayer—prayer, persistent, patient, determined; prayer that will take no denial; prayer that if it goes away one day unsatisfied, keeps on saying, "Well, there's tomorrow and tomorrow; God may wait to be gracious, and I can wait to receive, but receive I must and will." This is what the Bible means when it says, "The kingdom of heaven suffereth violence, and the violent take it by force." It does not say the eager, the impatient take it by force, but the violent—they who declare, "I will not let Thee go except Thou bless me." I must get down on my knees and own that I am less than nothing; seek God, not joy; consent to suffer, not cry for relief. And how transcendently good He is, when He brings me down to that low place, and there shows me that that self-renouncing, self-despairing spot is just the one where He will stoop to meet me.

SO BE IT

So be it; 'tis Thy plan not mine,
   And being Thine is good;
My God, my will shall yield to Thine
   Ere it is understood.

So be it; I a child of dust
   Will not oppose Thy way.
Move on, mysterious Will, I trust,
   I love, and will obey.

So be it; and do thou, my heart,
   No childish questions ask,
Thou in God's counsels hast no part,
   Crave not so hard a task.

So be it; yes, so be it, Lord,
   No word have I to say—
O be Thy gracious Name adored—
   I love, I will obey.

THOSE words, "daily nearer God," have an inexpressible charm for me. I long for such nearness to Him that all other objects shall fade into comparative insignificance; so that to have a thought, a wish, a pleasure apart from Him, shall be impossible.

THERE is one thing I can do, and that is to pray that Jesus would do for me what He did for the blind man—put His hands yet again upon my eyes and make me to see clearly.

I AM not sure that it is best for us, once safe and secure on the Rock of Ages, to ask ourselves too closely, what this and that experience may signify. Is it not better to be thinking of the Rock, not of the feet that stand upon it? It seems to me that we ought to be unconscious of ourselves, and that the nearer we get to Christ the more we shall be taken up with Him. We shall be like a sick man who, after he gets well, forgets all the symptoms he used to think so much of, and stops feeling his pulse, and just enjoys his health, only pointing out his physician to all who are diseased.

REST! What an infinite, mournful sweetness in the word; how perfectly sure I feel that my soul can never rest in itself, nor in anything of earth; if I find peace, it must be in the bosom of God.

I KNOW myself to be perfectly helpless. I cannot promise to do, or to be, anything; but I do want

to put everything else aside, and to devote myself
entirely to the service of Christ.

FAINT NOT

FAINT not beneath the loving Hand
  That wisely chastens thee,
Jesus will make thee understand
  Why this sharp stroke must be.

And if the pains are long drawn out,
  Oh, weary not, be strong,
Suffer in patience, Jesus' love
  Can do thy soul no wrong.

Honor the pangs that come from Him;
  Give thanks for pain and smart,
Thy groans and sighs have echoes found
  Within His sacred Heart.

Oh lonely Sufferer! oh, Lord,
  What agonies were Thine!
Give us, Thy followers, fellowship
  In sorrows so divine.

From Thine own bitter cup, let all
  Thy faithful children drink;
Start we not back like coward souls,
  Nor from Thy chastening shrink.

We love Thee, choose Thee, give to us
What first was given to Thee;
So shall we in Thy likeness grow,
And one in heart with Thee.

THE thorny path bears some of the sweetest flowers that adorn life; and when with naked, bleeding feet we walk upon a flinty soil, we often find diamonds.

A CUP of cold water given in Christ's name, if that is all one can give, is just as acceptable as the richest offering; and so is a teaspoonful, if one has no more to give. Christ loves to be loved; and the smallest testimony of real love is most pleasing to Him—and love shown to one of His suffering disciples, He regards as love to Himself. So a little child carrying a flower to some poor invalid, may thus do Christ honor and become more endeared to Him.

WEARINESS

AH is there, anywhere, a sorer heart
Than this sore heart of mine?
Jesus, have mercy on me, let me lay
Its griefs on Thine.

If Thou dost fail me, everything will fail;
    Pain be too hard to bear;
Then dost Thou pity me that I am sad?
    Lord, dost Thou care?

All eyes, save mine, may weep, but not for me
    Is the refreshing tear;
My tears are prayers, are speechless sighs and groans;
    O dost Thou hear?

Let my life be an all-day looking to Jesus. Let my love to God be so deep, earnest, and all-pervading, that I cannot have even the passing emotion of rebellion to suppress. There is such a thing as an implicit faith in, and consequent submission to, Christ. Let me never rest till they are freely mine.

There is no one, old or young, who has not the power of blessing other souls. We all have far more influence, both for good and evil, than we dream of.

I believe fully with you, that there is no happiness on earth, as there is none in heaven, to be compared with that of losing all things to possess Christ.

THERE may come a period when God says, virtu-
ally, to the soul, "You clung to Me when I smiled
upon and caressed you; let Me see how you will
behave when I smile and speak comfortably no
more."

SPEAK OF CHRIST

1.

OH speak to me of Christ! No name
    Falls on my ravished ear
With half the music, half the charm,
    That makes it bliss to hear
A loving voice pronounce that word
    As one who holds it dear.

2.

Hast thou not in some favored hour
    Beheld Him face to face,
And canst thou not make known to me
    Its beauty and its grace,
And lure me on to seek for Him
    In some familiar place?

3.

Hast thou not feasted on His word,
    And found it meat indeed;
And canst thou not a fragment spare
    On which my soul may feed—

Some promise, whispered by His lips,
    To meet my sorest need?

4.

Has He not revelations made
    In sacred hours to thee,
That thou canst hold as sacred trust,
    And yet confide to me
Who love, but fain would love Him more,
    Have seen, yet more would see?

5.

Yes, speak of Christ! As one who speaks
    Of his familiar friend,
As one who sees Him every day,
    May on His steps attend,
As one who oft, on reverent knee,
    Before Him loves to bend.

6.

Speak with a living warmth, a glow
    That shall my heart inflame,
And with thy rich and conscious love
    Put my poor love to shame,
Until I, too, have learned to speak
    That dearest, dearest Name.

THERE is a bright side to religion, and I love to see
Christians walking in the sunshine.

I CAN'T make myself sorry for Christ's disciples when He takes them in hand. He does it so tenderly, so wisely, so lovingly; and it can hardly be true, can it, that He is just as near and dear to me when my cup is as full of earthly blessings as it can hold, as He is to you, whose cup He is emptying? I have always thought they knew and loved Him best, who knew Him in His character of Chastiser, but perhaps one never loses the memory of His revelations of Himself in that form, and perhaps that tender memory saddens and hallows the day of prosperity. It matters very little on what paths we are walking, since we find Him in every one. How ashamed we shall be when we get to heaven, of our talk about our trials here!

Why don't we sing songs, instead? We know how, for He has put the songs into our mouths.

A blessed song of love to Thee,
Jesus, my Lord and King.

TO BE LIKE THEE

OH Jesus Christ, in self-despair
I come to Thee! Hear Thou the prayer
Laid at Thy feet; I leave it there—

To be like Thee!

Turn out the darling bosom-sin,
The love of self that rules within,
My earnest longing let me win—
    To be like Thee!

Oh let me see Thy lovely face,
Oh let me hear Thy words of grace,
In Thine own image grow apace—
    To be like Thee!

O Gentle, Sinless, Undefiled,
Ev'n in Thy justice meek and mild,
Help me, Thy loving, longing child—
    To be like Thee!

It would be pleasant to spend one's whole time among sufferers, and to keep testifying to them what Christ can and will become to them, if they will only let Him.

I am sure that He who has so sorely afflicted you accepts the patience with which you bear the rod, and that when this first terrible amazement and bewilderment are over, and you can enter into communion and fellowship with Him, you will find a joy in Him, that, hard as it is to the flesh to say so, transcends all the sweetest and best joys of human life. You will have nothing to do now but to fly to Him.

I have seen the time when I could hide myself in Him as a little child hides in its mother's arms, and so have thousands of aching hearts.

In all our afflictions He is afflicted.

May God bless and keep you, and fully reveal Himself to you.

"LORD, WHAT WOULDST THOU HAVE ME TO DO?"

Hast Thou, my Master, aught for me to do
    To honor Thee today?
Hast Thou a word of love to some poor soul,
    That I may say?

For see, this world that Thou hast made so fair,
    Within its heart is sad;
Thousands are lonely, thousands sigh and weep;
    But few are glad.

To which of them shall I stretch forth my hand,
    With sympathetic grasp?
Whose fainting form, for Thy dear sake, shall I
    Fondly enclasp?

They all are dear to Thee; and loving Thee,
    Dear are they all to me;
In every visage marred by grief and pain,
    Thy mark I see.

Straight from my heart, each day a blessing goes
    Warmly, through Thee, to theirs;
They are enfolded in my inmost soul,
    And in my prayers.

But which, among them all, is mine today?
    O guide my willing feet
To some poor soul that, fainting on the way,
    Needs counsel sweet.

Or into some sick-room where I may speak
    With tenderness of Thee;
And showing who and what Thou art, O Christ,
    Bid sorrow flee.

Or unto one whose straits call not for words;
    To one in want, in need;
Who will not counsel, but will take from me
    A loving deed.

Surely Thou hast some work for me to do!
    Oh, open Thou mine eyes,
To see how Thou wouldst choose to have it done,
    And where it lies!

WE love God more than we are aware; when He slays us, we trust in Him; when He strikes us, we kiss His hand.

THE PERFECT FRIEND

LORD, from myself, my faults, my sins
    Heart-sick to Thee I flee!
With each new day anew begins
    Folly's supremacy.

And from my dearest friends I fly—
    They err, they change, they fail;
My hopes they disappoint; well-nigh
    My faith in man assail.

To Thee I come! *Thou* canst not sin;
    I come to Thee for rest!
Oh, let a weary wanderer in,
    By sin and grief opprest!

Looking to Thee, Lord, day by day,
    Let me myself forget,
Meekly content to let Thee pay,
    Dear Lord, of sin my debt.

Looking to Thee with all the love
    Once to earth's treasures given,
Content to find, at last, above,
    Perfected friends in heaven!

MY EXPECTATION IS FROM THEE

LORD, I have nothing, in myself am naught,
　　Weak as a bruised reed Thou findest me;
And yet I dare to call myself Thy child,
　　Because my expectation is from Thee.

I am so poor in grace, so weak in faith,
　　Seek Thee so feebly on the bended knee;
And yet I must keep seeking, still aspire
　　Because my expectation is from Thee.

I long so for Thy presence, yet how oft
　　My sins constrain me from Thy face to flee;
I grieve, I falter, but hold on my way,
　　Because my expectation is from Thee.

I do the deeds I would not; leave undone
　　The gracious work that should completed be;
I am ashamed and sorry, yet hope on,
　　Because my expectation is from Thee.

And the dread enemy of my poor soul
　　Tempts me to yield and fail; but even he
Gives place at mention of Thy dearest name,
　　Because my expectation is from Thee.

So self-renouncing, desperate in myself,
　　My fallen ruins I can calmly see,

For when I poorest am, all lost and gone,
   My only expectation is from Thee.

THE longer I live the more conscious I am of human frailty, and of the constant, overwhelming need we all have of God's grace.

"AT EVENING-TIME THERE SHALL BE LIGHT"

AT evening-time there shall be light!
   Yes, when the night draws nigh,
When shadows lengthen, and the sun
   Is parting from the sky;
When the warm air grows chill, and earth
   Lies in obscurity;

There shall be light! a light unseen
   Amid the glare of day,
It shall illume the lonely path
   Through which thy footsteps stray,
To guide thee, lure thee, cheer thee on
   Amid the darkest way.

There shall be light! as tender hands
   Light children to their bed,
So shalt thou just as lovingly,

As tenderly be led,
And shown upon what pillow, thou
    Mayst lay thy weary head.

There shall be light! Yet faith's bright eye
    Alone that light can see;
Can take from death its chill, its gloom,
    And lend it ecstasy;
Look up! And see the risen Christ
    Shine, like the sun, for thee!

SOMETHING FOR CHRIST

SOMETHING for Thee! Lord, let this be
    Thy choice for me from day to day;
The life I live it is not mine,
Thy will, my will, have made it Thine!
    Oh, let me do in Thine own way,
        Something for Thee!

Something for Thee! What shall it be?
    Speak, Lord! Thy waiting servant hears,
Is it to do some mighty deed?
Is it some multitude to feed?
    Is it to do, 'mid pains and fears,
        Something for Thee?

Something for Thee! I do not see
    A coming battle for my King,

I only see a little cup—
With water, haste to fill it up.
   Thy love will own this trivial thing,
     Something for Thee!

Something for Thee! From self I flee,
   What wilt Thou, Master, from me still?
With eager heart I stand and wait,
Longing for work, or small or great:
   Let me be doing as Thy will,
     Something for Thee!

Something for Thee! On bended knee,
   Unseen, unknown, by mortal eye,
My soul for other souls shall plead—
As Thou for me didst intercede.
   Thy love can own a tear, a sigh,
     Something for Thee!

Something for Thee! Yet if for me
   It is a useless, crippled hand,
Let perfect patience mark my way.
Since they who silently obey
   Are doing as Thy wisdom planned,
     Something for Thee!

LET me press on through pain and loss,
Bending beneath my Master's cross,
Learning as they were taught.

Jesus, Beloved of my heart,
I feel Thine answer—mine Thou art.

"OH, COME THOU DOWN TO ME, OR TAKE ME UP TO THEE"

I WOULD be with Thee, dearest Lord, I long Thy face to see,
I long that each succeeding day should bring me nearer Thee;
Wilt Thou come down to dwell with me, wilt Thou with me abide;
Wilt Thou go with me where I go, be ever at my side?

Thy home is with the humble; Lord, that blessed truth I know;
But cannot change my heart myself; do Thou, then, make it so;
Oh come, my Saviour, come to me, it is not life to live,
Unless Thy presence fills my soul, except Thyself Thou give.

Or if Thou canst not come to me, a weak, a sinful child,
If Thou, alas, dost find in me no temple undefiled,
Oh then, my gracious Lord, send down a messenger for me,
And strip my sinfulness away and take me up to Thee.

I care not where I find Thee, Lord, whether or here
 or there,
I only know I want to find and love Thee, everywhere;
This world with all its tears and groans, would be my
 chosen place,
If Thou shouldst plan it for the scene in which to
 show Thy face.

And heaven with all its peace and rest, would be no
 heaven to me,
If I might dwell forever there, without a glimpse of
 Thee;
It is not life, or life's best joys, it is not heaven I want,
But oh, Thou risen Christ, for Thee, for Thee alone,
 I pant!

NOTES

NOTES

NOTES

Made in United States
Troutdale, OR
02/19/2024

17818678R00043